Gallery Books
Editor: Peter Fallon

SMASHING THE PIANO

John Montague

SMASHING THE PIANO

Gallery Books

Smashing the Piano
is first published
simultaneously in paperback
and in a clothbound edition
on 18 November 1999.

The Gallery Press
Loughcrew
Oldcastle
County Meath
Ireland

ISBN 1 85235 253 1 (*paperback*)
     1 85235 254 X (*clothbound*)

The Gallery Press acknowledges the financial assistance
of An Chomhairle Ealaíon / The Arts Council, Ireland,
and the Arts Council of Northern Ireland.

Contents

Fierce lyric truth,
Sought since youth,
Grace my ageing
As you did my growing,
Till time engraves
My final face.

'Twixt two extremes of passion, joy and grief.
— King Lear V, *iii*

for Donnell Deeny

Paths

We had two gardens.

A real flower garden
overhanging the road
(our miniature Babylon).
Paths which I helped
to lay with Aunt Winifred,
riprapped with pebbles;
shards of painted delph;
an old potato boiler;
a blackened metal pot,
now bright with petals.

Hedges of laurel, palm.
A hovering scent of boxwood.
Crouched in the flowering
lilac, I could oversee
the main road, old Lynch
march to the well-spring
with his bucket, whistling,
his carroty sons herding
in and out their milch cows;
a growing whine of cars.

Then, the vegetable garden
behind, rows of broad beans
plumping their cushions,
the furled freshness of
tight little lettuce heads,
slim green pea-pods above
early flowering potatoes,
gross clumps of carrots,
parsnips, a frailty of parsley,
a cool fragrance of mint.

Sealed off by sweetpea
clambering up its wired fence,
the goats' tarred shack
which stank in summer,
in its fallow, stone-heaped corner.

With, on the grassy margin,
a well-wired chicken run,
cheeping balls of fluff
brought one by one into the sun
from their metallic mother —
the paraffin incubator —
always in danger from
the marauding cat, or
the stealthy, hungry vixen:
I, their small guardian.

Two gardens, the front
for beauty, the back
for use. Sleepless now,
I wander through both
and it is summer again,
the long summers of youth,
as I trace small paths
in a trance of growth:
flowers pluck at my coat
as I bend down to help
or speak to my aunt
whose calloused hands
caressing the plants
are tender as a girl's.

Within

To open a door
and step into
a magic garden.
Childhood dreams
of it, somewhere
a gate hinge among

the tall flowers,
tangled creepers,
or a small knob
lost under petals.
No one watches as
you slowly push

that secret entrance
open, to escape from
those everlasting calls
of *Where are you?*
Come back home
at once, please!

❖

Orders, injunctions,
you will not hear
beyond that door
safe in the silence,
brushed by the hover-
ing wings of butterflies,

the same warm beauty
as on the outside, all
colour and movement,
leaves shifting, sighing,
a branch trembling
as though near speech.

❖

The air rinsed clear,
bright with potency,
as if some magic figure —
a stooped gardener,
or a friendly giant —
might suddenly appear,

but only the self
listening to the self,
awash with stillness,
taut with anticipation,
bright with awareness,
far from the botheration.

Fairy Fort

for Ben Simmons

As an immense privilege
he is brought down
to the underground hall
where all the giants
have been slumbering
since Time's beginning,

So long that their beards
have grown into the wood
of their big dining table.
Rascally, he cannot resist
a boastful hallooing:
*I am now younger and
stronger than you, you
big Numb Skulls!*

Rusty as treadmills
their great heads lift,
their beards tear away
from the rough planks,
their arms creak awake
to reach out defiantly again
for swords, for flagons.

And he flees backwards
through the cave's mouth.
But now all are gone:
princes, lords and curtsey-
ing ladies, pirouetting
to the fiddles' scraping.

Only the wet hedge
with, at the centre of
a lichened thorn bush,
a single bird singing
into the enormous silence
of the morning.

Still Life, with Aunt Brigid

Still nourished by her care
and love, which never seems to fail,
not only through ceaseless prayer
but like an attendant angel
sensed, a hovering fragrance
against the plainest of backgrounds;
as, crossing the cobbles at night,
on some last errand (are the hens
locked in safely, the calves foddered,
the yard gate looped closed?)
the swaying light of the stormlamp
or a hand-sheltered candle, flickers
around her frail figure, limned in gold
and shadows, like a Rembrandt.

Kindertotenlieder

TIME OFF

A bleaching sun on Rarogan Hill;
lifting the falling corn, plaiting the sheaves,
a man's work, but Martha bustles to please,
more at ease than in the schoolroom
where so often she extends an open palm.

The cattle suck the salt lick,
huddle under the trees, or break
clumsily wild while the triangle
of stubborn corn shrinks steadily before
the machine's shuddering teeth.

On the second day, she wilts,
complains of a brow bound in pain,
a heat blur before her eyes.
She is told to work on and,
when she fumbles, gruffly criticised.

The sun burns; the rain holds off.
The men are too intent to return
to the house for a cool drink, or aspirin.
The reaper is hired and, as it rattles
and races to bite the stalks,

the sheaves are still to bind.
At twilight Martha slumps like a grain sack.
They trudge her heavy body home.
For three days they cannot return.
Even a child's funeral takes time.

CROSSROADS

The dead silence
of extreme heat.

The elements for tragedy:
a country crossroads
where a young man
might meet & quarrel
with a stranger, or
take a left turn, and
land in the dungeon

(or the right, and love
the lovely princess;
my own plan, later).
Rarely, straight on.

Take that crossroads,
where three townlands
meet, Altcloghfin,
Roscavy, Rarogan,
at Garvaghey churchyard.

Mid-August, mid-'30s,
the spill of the spring
dwindles to a trickle.
The wayside flowers
are furred with dust.
Thick leaves hang.

A smell of thunder.
Few people stir out,
but young MacDonald

gets his leg under
his father's Raleigh.
He wobbles through Altcloghfin
and finds there is a cooling wind
as he freewheels down
Garvaghey's long incline

to swoop out into
the middle of the crossroads
straight into the path
of a suddenly swerving
and rubber-shredding,
furiously braking big car.

(Sam Clark had an errand.
He is driving from Belfast to Derry.
Because of the swelter
all his windows are open.
Because the road is deserted
he puts the foot down.)

News of the accident
crackles like gorsefire
through the torpid countryside:
A schoolboy killed
at Garvaghey crossroads!

Voices, anxious, loud,
call me in from the fields,
call and call, until
I come racing, racing in.
Now what have I done?

I thrust a scared face
around the byre corner
to be hailed with relief:
Thank God, you're safe.

Then go back to whack
the heads off the thistles,
throw stones at the magpies
(or lie in the haybarn
and dream of the princess).

While, in the dead silence
of extreme heat, a schoolmate's
mangled body is gathered
away into an ambulance,
leaving behind the taped
and chalk-measured
scene of an accident:
a problem abandoned
on a school blackboard.

Prayers for My Daughters

for Oonagh and Sibyl

LE BAIN
An Answer to Balthus

No odalisque of weaving bodies,
luxurious harems of Delacroix,
Carthaginian splendours of *Salammbo*,
a satin-rich chamber of sensualities,

only my two small daughters, play-
ing happily in their bath, pleased
with their chubby bodies, as they romp
amongst the suds, seal-slippery with soap:

such throaty giggles at being naked,
such delight in being animal-alive,
with so many years still to come
as a rubber duck hides under a bum

or a plastic flotilla advances in a mock war;
then the sobering pitcher of tepid water,
the rough pleasure of being towelled until
you are toast-warm and glowing all over!

GUARDIANS

In my sick daughter's room
the household animals gather.
Our black Tom poses lordly on
the sun-warmed windowsill.
A spaniel sleeps by her slippers,
keeping one weather eye open.
For once, they agree to differ:
nary a sound, or spit of bother.
Aloof and hieratic as guardians,
they seem wiser than this poor animal,
her father, tiptoeing in and out,
ferrying water-bottle, elixirs, fruit,
his unaccustomed stockinged stealth
tuned anxiously to a child's breath.

LAST CHANCE

'All the other children at school
keep saying Santa doesn't exist,'
my thoughtful Sibyl tests.

'And what do you think yourself?'
I probe, sensing an Ulster advantage,
pruning a small household expense.

'Well, I do wonder, sometimes,
how he scrambles down our chimney,
since we built up the fireplace.

And I never hear the clatter
of his high black boots, or
the neigh of the nine reindeer.

And how do his team fly, without wings?'
She opens small arms, questioning.
'So maybe we'll skip this year?'

Doubt clouds her face,
then first cunning. 'But, Daddy,
I didn't say that *I* didn't believe.

So let's leave the back door open
to give him a last chance and
if he doesn't show up this time,

then he really is a dream.'

THE SICK BIRD

I

Cycling along the Clogher road
Master MacGurren found a sick bird.
He brought it to me, sick in bed,
and it lay, in a rag-lined shoe box,
within reach of my caressing hand.

After a few days, it learnt to respond
to the touch of a warm finger
on its fragile head, bruised feathers.
Its claws were crisp as winter twigs
and its small heart hammered:
minute, intense, terrible.

One morning I was better, and
so was my little companion, hungry
beak gaping on the pillow beside me.
I cupped it in my palms and,
cradling it to the window, hoisted
and helped it fly away.

II

Thirty years later, I find a bird
on the road's edge, outside Ballydehob:
a coal tit, *meantán dubh*.
I place its delicate body inside
my shirt, as I cycle home,
to show it to my children.

Now it rests on the unlit stove
in a cushioned box, beside where I write,
inspected, every so often, by tiptoeing children.
Its heart is still furiously beating;
when will it take flight?

Between

for Michael Viney

That deep, dark pool. To come upon it,
after driving across the Gap in midsummer,
the hedges freighted with fuchsia, hawthorn,
blood-red and white under shining veils of rain.

A wind flurry finecombing the growing grain
as a full-uddered cow precedes us along the lane,
a curious calf poking its lubberly head over stone
while the country road winds betwixt and between.

Sudden, at the summit of the Knockmealdowns,
a chill black lake, a glacial corrie or tarn,
some large absence, hacked, torn
from the far side of the dreaming cliff.

A brooding silence, a hoarded font of nothing,
lightless, still, opaque . . . severely alone.
Except when a shiver, a skirl of wind
makes the waters tremble, mild as that field of grain.

But on the shorn flank of the mountain,
a flowering, flaring bank of rhododendron,
exalted as some pagan wedding procession.
Fathomless darkness, silent raging colour:

A contrast to make your secret self tremor,
like a child cradled in this quarry's murmur,
delighted but lost between the dark, the blossoming.
On one side, a moorland's bareness, rufous heather

Sheltering a long-nebbed curlew, bog asphodel or lobelia
and, on the other, that terraced orchestra of colour,
avenues of lavish amethyst blossom.
Chill of winter: full warmth of summer,

colliding head on in stillness, and a heavy aroma.

The Current

I saunter down to Sarah Bailey's empty house;
some spinster, enshrined in local history
for living, solitary as a heron, or some
other bogpool-haunting creature
in this dank, small-windowed, loosely
mortared stone nest by the ceaseless rush
of the Garvaghey river . . .

                                    Walls piled
with straw, it provides winter shelter
for cattle who bruise their warm backs
against each other, as I enter stealthily,
my feet crackling on the strewn fodder,
or sinking into fetlocked depths of dung, mud,
of what was once her clay floor. Other boys
and I met here, to share sticky sweets
and cigarettes (a *cache* behind a loose stone),
plotting devilment, away from home,
away from parents. And it was nearby
I first learnt a mystery, as everyone must,
striking matches against the encroaching dark.

An older boy leads me aside, crawling
down a tunnel of dragging brambles,
a thicket of thorn, and bruise-coloured sloes
to a dense ledge, overlooking our river
where bog-brown water pours endlessly over
a waterfall's lip, whirling into frothy spittle.
We lie down on a pelt of emerald moss,
littered with twigs, resinous bark, speckled insects,
already rusting fronds of fern, sorrel,
watercress, clover.

I trust him:
we have carried water from the same spring,
worked on the high bog. I watch
as he fumbles one by one the large metal buttons
of his dungarees, to uncover
a grotesque object, his much bigger cock,
its hammer head swollen with blood,
from which he draws the sheathe back,
to show the raw flesh, nakeder than naked,
already glistening with threads of liquid.

A sight familiar from any jakes wall
but awesome to me as he wrinkles it
back and forward with an urging hand,
working the membrane of the foreskin,
a blue vein beating along the length of it,
from the tender, tightening bag of the balls
to that small moist eye, the slit

                                    which gapes
like a gill, as he groans, gropes, and sighs.
Then his face stiffens, as though in pain,
his body goes rigid. Something new happens,
something I never dreamt or seen.
He shivers full length, and spills, shudders
some unknown white substance on the soft grass,
and I *must* watch as eerie, carnal-smelling sperm
drenches, mingles its warm, strange odour
of straw and loam, with the wildflowers
across our hiding place.

                        (After a while,
we will talk of girls, courting, future loves?
He will fold away his now-shrunken cock,
or I will dare display my still slender effort,

which I rub a little, without much effect.
Surely not the worst way to approach
love's central act, through friendship?)

But now he lies exhausted, spent,
as a gasping fish on the riverbank.
opposite. We do not touch, rest quiet,
but, between us, over the moss,
shine the snail tracks of a secret,
with, in the background, the hidden,

Overheard, pull and swirl of the current.

Dark Rooms

WRATH

Lying in the darkness, grim with anger

against the one lying by your side,
herself, grim with anger
at your lying
so grim with anger by her side.

This night only absence will be her lover,
only wrath will be your bride.

NIGHTJAR

Sleeplessness, a nightjar,
my familiar, sharply crying.

The bed becomes a boat,
mounting a dark stream;

To reach out and take
your hand across space,

a weakness, as the current
laps blackly beneath.

LYING FIGURE

I have never ceased to love you since that hotel room
where, naked, head averted, you cried, *Clear out*;
I can no longer remember our quarrel, my fault,
only the wallpaper, your curved back,
the day's still life, in that wardrobe mirror,
and my stunned belief, standing there,
that I would see you again.

after Michel Deguy

STAND IN

Devious candour waits
outside the bedroom door
until love is done, then

hobbles forward, slyly,
to inform you how one
told a white lie, how on

that marvellous night
when the brimming moon
silvered everything to dream

(the bed's white foam
in which her suddenly naked
body plunged and swam)

one heart beat untrue:
yes, she sighed for someone,
but no, it was not you,

those wild cries were for him,
her shadow lover, for whom you were
but a simulacrum, a stand in.

THE BLADE

In sleep, the pain is almost gone.
Only a vague fretting, on the edge
of consciousness, an animal
locked out, whimpering to be let in.
Then a slow concurrence of dark images
pools into dream. You wake again
to what you had forgotten.
The blade of loss begins to turn.

POSTSCRIPT

A fuel fiercer than love: bitterness!
As I bend to this long neglected page
in my stonecold attic, another, younger man
bends to your brown face: another less
mottled hand reaches out to cover yours
which lately lay so warm in mine
now desperately trying to forge a line
where furious, calm, I can control my rage,
wrestle my pain so as to take up again
my old-fashioned courtly poet's pilgrimage
towards the ideal, woman or windmill;
seething inside, but smiling like a sage.

CHAIN LETTER

Love letters, like messages, telegrams
from a more real world. You write
or read them, elated, trembling,

then stumble across them, moons later,
bundled in a corner, in a drawer,
where you had hidden, or dropped them,

as you might a tingling live wire
after the shock has flooded your veins,
and you scramble back to your daily situation.

Or buried in the proverbial stray volume
hoping the bulk of the pages might deaden
that raw pulse of exposed feeling.

And now, to come upon them, all over again,
a different, 'a sadder and a wiser man',
bemused by the fury of these wild lines

to someone changed, estranged, or gone.

Honey Harvest

The bee sways on the petal,
cargoed with sweetness.

(Little winged fellow,
where do you come from?)

I have flown from afar
to probe tenderly and explore
your velvet interior, delect-
ing your nectar.

(And I answer, savour
your hovering presence,
body I burnish with pollen
as you blunder and thrust:
then leave, carrying my elixir,
my benison, near and far.)

So year by year, honey
collects in clammy cells,
structured chambers of sweetness;
mansions of amber light,
city towers by night.

(Other flowers will blossom
from my scattered essence,
as bees of small strength tread
the flower harvest with their feet.)

When may I see you again?

The world sways on its axis
before such a tender question.
Love has all, has no rights.

(I hear your coming flight.)

Brighid O'Neill

Brighid O'Neill, no lie that you're lovely,
and I know for a fact you've scattered thousands of men;
but if you were beside me, after all this commotion,
sweet-voiced you'd be as, on her nest, the wren.

Waterfalling hair, pooled on her nape,
gay glance agleam like the morning dew,
sweet brow and cheeks, hourglass shape,
chalk-white breasts, veined milk blue.

Her purling, curling locks like gold leaf,
her tender, slender waist have always arrested me;
her lime-white thighs, her rowan-red cheeks;
whole hosts have been slain by Brighid O'Neill.

after the Irish

Talking with Victor Hugo, in Old Age

Late at night, you seek to explain your life,
set out what happened, how much you feel
you have achieved, and such inestimables . . .

(and I saw the Pléiade editions
in their missal binding, burning on the shelves,
so many noble volumes!).

Speaking with a grim surety and sorrow
of how, now, time is flowing
and the innermost heart slows
and its flaws
show.
      Confessing, finally, how
no matter the height and depth
of a man's achievement, the cogs and gears
of love and longing, of desire and heartbreak,
still lumber and thunder creakingly on;
like an old-fashioned threshing machine:

How, despite your great age,
your public dignity — Victor Hugo,
after your exemplary exile in Jersey,
living in your own lifetime
in a Paris avenue named after you!

There is no protection
against your predelictions;
love still a terrible thorn,
your weakness, not only ongoing,
but growing, passion
racking your frailing body,
a shuddering storm.

There are Days

for Lawrence Sullivan

There are days when
one should be able
to pluck off one's head
like a dented or worn
helmet, straight from
the nape and collarbone
(those crackling branches!)

and place it firmly down
in the bed of a flowing stream.
Clear, clean, chill currents
coursing and spuming through
the sour and stale compartments
of the brain, dimmed eardrums,
bleared eyesockets, filmed tongue.

And then set it back again
on the base of the shoulders:
well tamped down, of course,
the laved skin and mouth,
the marble of the eyes
rinsed and ready
for love; for prophecy?

Dumbshow

You'll have to run down to the shop:
my head dips, a dumbshow of assent,
as my aunt pens out the lengthening list
of articles no longer found on our musty shelf.

Windswift as Wilson, the *Wizard*'s sprinting star,
I whip down the always widening Broad Road,
then huddle, hang around, hesitate in the dark
cavern at the back of Kelly's newer shop.

Until there is no one left, and then I try
to fishgasp something, but in the end
just push forward the scribbled grocery list
and nod eagerly, as each item is cleared off.

A gas lamp hangs its hissing circle
over the flitches of lean and back bacon,
ropes of sausages, thick-crusted bread;
and all those words thronged in my head.

Every time I stand forth, fluent-tongued
in some foreign place, before an audience,
I am haunted, dogged by that mute lad,
as, warmly introduced, I step from the darkness.

Poor Poll

Snarled in misery, flailing animal;
a lord of language,
lockjawed in ice.

Others giggle as
he fails, stumbles,
pushes a consonant
slowly uphill, topples
into the bottomless
well of a vowel,
trips over dentals,
spits fricatives.

Syllable to syllable,
a tight-roped abyss;
a needless dolour
stains his years:
an act — simple as
walking — bulks, baulks,
large as a hurdle.

His dream to stride
fluently through
fields of language,
possible only when
his pen hand stirs
and ink spider-
webs on white.

Captain Greacen

for his seventieth birthday

Robert Greacen, I read you forty years ago,
'A servant girl's letter to her faithless lover',
or, more chillingly, that bird at the window,
'a black face of black, unknowing death';
a fine elegy for your Presbyterian father.

Both in the anthology gathered with Iremonger,
first of its kind, which we studied in Dwyers,
the Green Bar, or high-ceilinged Hartigans,
warmly disputing, away from the UCD classrooms;
Cronin declaiming 'Raftery's Dialogue with the Whiskey'.

Those were hard years, *On the Barricades*,
seeking to bring new verse to an old country,
which hid its ignorant head under its wing:
The Bell tolling: 'there are no young men appearing',
or 'the native stock was running pretty thin'.

A thumbs down from New York-based Padraic Colum,
unaware that a new atoll was quietly forming;
(was yours the orange red or pink corallium?).
Our gratitude then, for grafting in a hard time,
to hang in, like Captain Fox, a wily veteran.

The Yachtsman's Jacket

a portrait of Edward McGuire, RHA

Eddie, old friend, gone to the shades,
we both walked a while on the wild side.
You endeared yourself to me first
as you swayed above your father's swimming pool
and proclaimed: 'Let's have a piss!'

Two golden arcs in the Blackrock night.
Viking berserk, your drinking bouts:
wrecking Garech Browne's tiny mews flat
in a fracas with Dominic Behan,
angry, after you had upended Kathleen.

And I was crashing a party in Sandymount
when you came hurtling, backwards, out;
you stopped to say, 'Hello, John', then
lowered your head to charge in again,
waving your weapon, a bottle of stout.

Your humour as wayward as your anger.
Standing beside Barrie Cooke in P. Pye's flat
when Barrie, per usual, rippled a fart,
you unfolded your lean height, to declare:
'Picasso, perhaps, but a scruffy painter from Clare

has no right to poison my air.'
Behind all the rattle, awkwardly shy,
the unhealed hurt of a mother's boy,
all that lostness wrought to tension, fury
of contemplation, schemes of colour harmony,

the sitter's face, the leaf at the window.
Your Freudian trademark: that spiky dead bird.
Though you were gentle as you were wild,
charting the glooms of our middle-class Bohemia,
but also tender portraits of a girl child.

In due course, I joined your gallery,
to be received with old world courtesy,
before we clambered to your studio:
the draped camera, plus the green visor
to enable you concentrate on your task.

It was rainy and cold when I left,
so you settled your sailor's jacket
over my shoulders. 'I won't need it,'
you expostulate gently. Its bulk protects
me still, as I trudge fields of West Cork.

Claddagh Raga

The big house winks over
the sound, alluring you;
as does that tiny thatched
cottage by a rocky lake.

To join the wild gang
brandied to oblivion,
ladies squealing for congress
in sumptuous bedrooms?

Or let the woman of the cottage
bring you the blue duck-egg
while her man goes to fetch
unclouded poteen from the thatch?

Ways and worlds you
might inhabit, lurching
between sophistication
and innocence, while an

intrigued public lends an ear,
enchanted by such long-
delayed, luxuriantly
sustained ambivalence.

Robert, Old Stager

1

Where do they hail from,
the old high ones?
A fragrance plays around them,
the warm scent of freedom
that long, hard hours have won,
in cluttered studio, or bookroom.
In an ageing face still smoulders
the eager obstinacy of the young.

2

The last time I saw you
was under a blossoming apple tree
in a garden in central London.
Beneath that black bullfighter's hat
beamed your still mischievous smile:
a heartening example of how
to live with the muse, in style.

3

Robert, old stager,
now I can understand your anger,
so low-down, old-fashioned, and mean.
It was meant to gut
the false, to illustrate
how one could not be bought,

however high the price
or public the esteem:

It was a roaring shield
to protect our dream.

Summer School

Why does he appear, so abruptly,
ruffling my poise, as I launch
into a lecture on the later Yeats?
It is as if the old man himself
shoves and shivers the slates
of my skull, a dusty rook
crowing and cawing . . . *Young man,*

Be disrespectful, say what you will
of me: pompous as a high priest,
prophet-strident, with tuneless harsh voice
and half-mad eyes. Boring old W. B.
with his thickening senatorial waist,
pontificating about pernes and gyres,
the Great Wheel, and purgatorial fires!

I grasp the lectern, straighten
my papers, struggle to retain
my balance, only to hear again
that old-fashioned, chanting, Sligo voice,
calling on us all — pundits,
pedants, poets — to rejoice!

1971

In the Pool

In the pool at Versailles
the King's carp turns and turns;
he hears policy debates above him,
war on the greater waters
with England, Holland, Spain:
the Armada foundering off Ireland.

The courtiers' faces change;
a weed-laced beauty peers in,
sighing or swooning, on some enfolding arm.
Monarchs pass, even the great Sun King.
Favourites grow old, another beauty reigns.
Dynasties pass: Bourbon, Orleans.

Centuries dim, but I swim on.

A New Art

On the way towards a new art
she halts where the ochre earth
drinks warmth all day, to turn
towards evening, a flaring red.

The sparkle of this dry light
breeds wisdom, where herb and moth
blend fragrances, and the cricket
rubs its metal legs against the night.

On Hearing Kamaladevi Speak Again

A timeless voice stumbles on;
she chides us for our lack of imagination:
we always knew the atom could be broken,
but nothing perishes: something lives on.
It curves back again: complete break never comes.

Now we are free of earthbound history,
we need no longer slaughter the bison,
or stain the cave walls with crimson.
Scarcely breathing, she speaks of inspiration.
We stand in a black, starlit womb of creation.

Araby, 1984

Hot colours and confusions of Bombay Airport;
emigrant workers queuing for Dubai, Kuwait:
as the sun climbs, we board our flying carpet.

Another journey outwards, another heartening return
to our dancing children, as the *Morning Jewel*,
the airline's flagship, shadows lost Babylon.

That barrier of mountains is lone wolf Kurdistan.
Soon the Golden Horn: Constantinople or Byzantium,
the disputed glitter of Sophia's dome.

How shrunken seems the globe we turn upon:
graph of a world brain, or old chaos come again,
despite the saffron robes of holy men?

Our ship glides above it all as in a dream,
a mayfly light on the Heraclitean stream,
as you rest your head's gilt casket on my arm.

Sun Hymn

High summer, and Fota Island is in bloom,
flowering cherry and glow of rhododendron;
on country hedges, a fragrant cargo of hawthorn.

Flagrant or hidden, the power of the sun,
life-giving force, constantly streaming down.
In the evening, his consort mirrors him.

St John's Eve, bonfires curl to heaven.
Day star, *fáinne geal*, Sol, Hyperion,
all cultures bear witness to your warm

kindling at the heart of our creation.
Egyptian Ra or Re, lord of the pantheon,
scarab burning the sands he shines upon.

Dying each evening, born each flaming dawn,
over stark hillsides of Greece, blue Aegean,
Helios rolls the gold chariot of the sun,

white horses trained by his father, Hyperion,
upon steep, cloud-shrouded, Olympus mountain.
A change of scene; our Lord is born,

a light descending to transfix the Virgin,
a light illuminating the cave at Bethlehem,
where smiles a child, the Christian Sun.

Heart of grace, Dantean mandala of the universe,
where the large rose windows marry light and space
in the medieval cathedrals, the gentle furnace

of his burning love lightens the earth.
Bourges, Notre Dame, Sainte Chapelle, Chartres,
celebrate this glorious dying and re-birth,

which happens so casually for us each day
as the sun pursues his heavenly pathway,
bestowing its grave light, almost indifferently.

While ceaselessly the cloud cattle saunter by
where on Fota, a blue mirror gathers the sky,
transforming light into the pulse of energy.

A slanting cathedral roof for the space age,
a small sun temple, child of Stonehenge,
harnessing for us the sun's pretended rage:

gold band of eternity, wedding ring of reality,
Andean ingot of glory, paschal candle of the sky,
flame at the heart of mystery, our system's burning eye.

A Charm for Europe

for Anise Koltz

Sometimes, a glimmer of a shape,
the faintest shadow of a hope,
as we regard our first and last step.

The plunging beasts of Lascaux,
ample buttocks of the Lespuge Venus,
ornate helmet of a Geat warrior:

Men lunging to slaughter bison,
or lured by nature to procreation;
then the homage, to brute courage,

to comradeship, to love's elation:
a song rising in the tired evening,
Luth of *provencal*, scop's Anglo-Saxon.

❖

Through the landscape a river runs
and sites spring up, small at first,
expanding through centuries into cities.

Tiber, Danube, Seine, *sweete Themmes*,
Rome, Vienna, Paris and London:
a blessing on all who crowd in them.

Protect them from old taints of war;
even God's word a terrible sword,
Eastern or Roman, Luther's just anger,

disputed frontiers and fraternal murder.
A broken Europe with its torn borders
lures us to a less bloody future.

❖

Shrunken now, no longer the world's centre,
the mighty Roman or British empire,
but in our shared weakness, a mother

who has mourned her sons too long,
who has seen her fields sprout skeletons,
and now seeks a way beyond that burden

of the harsh blunders we call history:
neither strong nor weak, but weary
of discords, heart-sick for harmony.

Sonnet on the Opening of Wrixon's Wine Cellar

Arrayed, they drowse on their flanks,
slender-throated bottles of Burgundy, Bordeaux,
slowly mellowing in cobwebbed, umbral silence
before we broach their tilted necks.
They dream of burgeoning upon the vine,
nourished by the soil, the sun, the rain:
empurpled Cabernet, effervescent Vouvray,
the lusty, florid Chinon of Rabelais.
Wine, the new empire, garlanding the earth,
with all the noble rottenness of grape
stored in cask or vat or magnum shape
to slake our thirst, provoke our mirth,
till we are drawn into the dance by Bacchus,
wreathed in vine leaves, smiling upon us.

The Two Seáns

SEÁN Ó RÍORDÁIN

Hermit crab of
a receding language

(an eye protrudes
from under the ledge
of his scalloped hat)

a carapace above
his lopsided
crinkled smile

Malice rears
its serpent head
but like robed Chinese
we greet and bow

(hovering from one foot
to another, on Oliver Plunkett
Street in Cork, opposite
the Five Star Supermarket,
intent but diffident)

custodians of different
areas of the same strand
specialists of decline
connoisseurs of solitude.

SEÁN Ó RIADA

Along a lonely country road
in the Gaeltacht
striding through warm sunlight
you walk past

a small old woman
singing to herself
as she sidles along
in the opposite direction.

You salute her, gravely,
perhaps lift your hat
but she does not smile
as she glides by

and only after she has passed
does a chill tell you
that beneath her shawl
she had no shoes,

and no feet, but was floating
a foot above the ground!
You turn quickly around
but there is no one to be found.

Along that lonely country road
beneath Mount Brandon.

Sweet & Sour

1

If you strung a rosary, girl,
for every man you brought to bed,
from what I hear, Miss O'Neill,
you'd soon run out of thread.

2

There's a girl from these parts —
never mind her name —
and the force of her farts
is like flailing grain.

3

O nice young lady, don't think you're smart
with all that gear your breed never had:
they'd prefer a milch herd on a mountainside
to a fancy petticoat on a broad backside.

4

Old pal, don't mock my rampaging;
King David had a hundred in his old age.
It's disrespectful to say of that great king
that the young women found his machinery creaking.

after the Irish

Starspill

That secret laughter
which, on bad days,
keeps us buoyant,
awaiting the hidden
glitter of accident.

White waves breaking
beneath Mount Eagle;
a guardian, mist-veiled?
No lift in the sky,
no glow behind it:
a fierce rain spitting
as we reach Brandon
for a lost day's drinking.

Beyond midnight I push
open the stubborn pub door
to confront a full moon,
and a spill of stars
across a sky opaque
and black as a bog pool:
dice strewn across
a table of velvet.

Raptors

an answer to Leopardi

CONSERVATIVES
'e fango e il mondo'

Let us not forget to celebrate
Nature's strangeness. The serrated
length of the terrible predators,
the childish waddle of Sister Alligator,
the splendid torpor of Brother Crocodile,
nearly indistinguishable from his warm mud.

With all of us worshipping the same God!
Praise their thick conservative skins,
pay homage to their enormous jaws,
creaking open, like prison doors,
as some shy beast comes teetering
in dawn light, to the waterhole . . .

NATURE

'. . . la natura, il brutto
Poter che, ascoso, a comun danno impera . . . '

Walking that morning
we found a trapped
animal that had gnawed
off half its leg
to escape, and did
with a final thrust
as we approached,
but couldn't hobble far
before it was caught
and savaged by our terrier.

I rescued it from
her trained mouth
and held it up.
Now an eye was gone
as well as a hind leg.
The natural world has
no begging bowl and
our bitch was waiting.
I let it fall back.

BALOR

A fierce gullet yawns.
A black brow, thick black hair
matting the knuckles.
Eternally open, unsleeping,
a lidless staring eye
exudes its baleful force.

Padding back and forth
in the cage of your mind,
you sweat a monster's unease.
We must yield to the damp power
you conjure from your exhaustion;
— yield or perish!

But I listen, wary
of that whistling void,
the grave under the tongue:
that cannibal darkness
which underlies everything,
killing and eating.

Ravenous, you strike against
bars of your hammering
that now stretch out between us,
plotting our different truths,
black against white,
darkness against light.

Remission

for François Simon

With wife and daughter this evening
you receive us, smiling, although
paralysed from the waist down, and
hauled from the electric wheelchair
to your own table by helpful hands.

Yet splashing out your best wine
into your guest's glass, or handing
round the plates, you deride the pain
your racked body feels, proclaim the joy
of being allowed some normal time again,

to be hailed, to converse as a friend,
not a special case. Constant humiliation
of the body has brought your Johnsonian
brow to bulge with hard-won vision,
the manic gleam of almost blessing.

Soon we will creak you away from the table,
ferry and wheel you back from your home
to your institution room again. Leaving,
I will take both your hands in mine,
although in neither have you any feeling.

Dear specialist in waste, professor of pain,
with your feebled body, pierced as a pin-cushion,
you still persist, as if beyond such sickness,
even beyond death's encroaching ruin,
there dwelt some final, lasting sweetness.

Flower, Stone, Sea

'The flower that splits the rocks'
                    — William Carlos Williams

THE SMELL OF THE EARTH

At Carnac, the smell of the earth
has something not recognisable.

It is an odour of earth
perhaps, but transferred
to the level of geometry.

Where the wind, the sun, the salt,
the iodine, the bones, the sweet water of streams,
the dead seashells, the grasses, the slurry,
the saxifrage, the warmed stone, the bilge,
the still-wet linen, the tar of boats,
the byres, the whitewashed walls, the fig trees,
the old clothes of the people, their speech,
and always the wind, the sun, the salt,
the slightly disgusting loam, the dried seaweed,

all together and separately struggle
with the epoch of the menhirs

to measure up.

                    after Guillevic: CARNAC

FLOWERS

Carnac

Majesty should not
go unaccompanied.
In the crevice of
a rock at Carnac
I found a small
blue flower —
a harebell.
Fed by flying
spume and rain
it flourished in its pocket
of dour granite;
a child clutching
a giant's arm.

Rocamadour

A gold medallion
graces her dark neck

the line of the body
a sturdy promontory

warmed and hollowed
by tidal centuries

to hold a solemn child
wholly human, wholly god

a flower, crevice-lodged
under a cliff of wood.

AT TEILHARD DE CHARDIN'S GRAVE

A Jesuit graveyard recalls a military cemetery,
small white stones standing to attention,
orderly as that other trim forest of the dead,
the white crosses glooming above the Somme,
awaiting the mute trumpet of the resurrection.

French aristocrat, bearer of the ennobling *de*,
you now lie between MacQuade and Reilly,
foot-soldiers in the army of Jesus;
you who were earth's theologian,
servant of the evolving logos, who sought
in Chinese deserts to decipher
the living book of our universe.

A gaunt calvary broods on a hillock
above you and your fallen comrades:
three veiled and mourning women
the shadowy figure of an exhausted Christ;
the dead centre of your world as priest.

In winter there are tracks through the snow
to your grave. In summer, flowers.
Each evening the last rays of the sun
strike your tomb, above 'the lordly Hudson'.

LULLABY

3 September 1963

Great sea-mother, your voice
is monotonous! I sat beside
you for a whole day, trying
to speak of a friend's death,
but all that you answered
was one single word,
with its many variations . . . *S-h-u-s-h.*

THE WELL-WROUGHT URN

Ancient vessels were ceremonial,
lofted by druid, rabbi, priest.
Once the temple of the body shone
like the dwelling of the Holy Ghost.
A lonely vigil before the altar
cleansed the knight for his quest.
In the silence of the ornate urn
princely dust was laid to rest.
Now such rites fade, spectral
as a chrome or plastic vessel.
Part spirit, we long for past ritual.
Brightness of flowers on a lit table
ignites memories of goblet, grail:
each petal powerful, still, frail.

The Family Piano

My cousin is smashing the piano.
He is standing over its entrails
swinging a hatchet in one hand
and a hammer handle in the other
like a plundering Viking warrior.

My cousin is smashing the piano
and a jumble, jangle of eighty-eight keys
and chords, of sharps and flats
clambers to clutch at the hatchet,
recoils, to strike at his knees

(*My cousin is smashing the piano!*)
like the imploring hands of refugees
or doomed passengers on the *Titanic*
singing 'Nearer My God to Thee'
as they vanish into lit, voiceless seas.

My cousin is smashing the piano
Grandfather installed in the parlour
to hoop his children together.
It came in a brake from Omagh,
but now lists, splintered and riven.

My cousin is smashing the piano
where they gathered to sing in chorus
'My Bonny Lies Over The Ocean'
beneath the fading family portraits
of Melbourne Tom, Brooklyn John.

My cousin is smashing the piano
where buxom Aunt Winifred played
old tunes from scrolled songbooks,
serenely pressing the pedals, and singing
'Little Brown Jug', 'One Man Went to Mow',

Or (*My cousin is smashing the piano*)
hammered out a jig, 'The Irish Washerwoman',
while our collie dog lifted its long nose
and howled to high heaven:
John Cage serenading Stockhausen!

Looking Glass

Combing her long hair out, like some heroine
from the Fenian tales, my aunt, Mary O'Meara,
confronting her bedroom mirror in Abbeylara;
her hair was greying, but still plentiful,
thick and burnished as a horse's mane
beneath those slow, luxurious strokes,

Myself, perched by her side, a motherless boy,
fascinated by the crackle of static electricity,
(a Brooklyn trolley swaying, sparks flying, lickety-
split; or clickety-clack, knitting needles clashing),
the way she tossed its heavy length back,

Or, mumbling through a mouthful of hairpins,
ransacked her memory to amuse me:
her Old World courtship, her favourite story;
the way the young Waterford schoolmaster
came down the valley from his post in Rarogan
to visit her, in her father's house, in Garvaghey:

'He used sit beside me, where you are now,
watching intently: my hair was chestnut brown,
my crowning glory, he gallantly called it;
one day, in the mirror, I saw his hand reach out
and almost touch it: our love's first secret.'

The Straying Blackthorn

Rummaging in the attic, I come upon
my maternal grandfather's walking stick,
a knobbly blackthorn, with a metal tip
and a round polished top, that still fits
snugly into the palm. Was Granda Carney
a hero to swing such a monstrous bludgeon,
striking skull or road an echoing thwack?

I subscribe briefly to such a mythical ancestor,
fit to be an Ulster poet's grandfather,
but penitently remember the homelier truth:
he was a small man, afeard of the wife
who locked him away, to halt drinking bouts.
Seeking to squeeze through the top back window
he slid down the spout, into the water butt!

Still, to this day, a sobering thought.
I bore it proudly off, but unused to the heft
left it behind me in Heathrow Airport.
Imagine some brisk British business man
in his boardroom armour of collar and bowler,
some sweeping Sikh, or bemused porter,
running a light hand down this gnarled object

and pondering what, under heaven, to do with it?
Or perhaps it sailed off to some foreign port
to become the big stick of an African chief
among his manifold wives, holding court,
or wafted on Concorde by a briefcased diplomat.
Drifting through space, my mind's eye follows it,
Fintona's first missile, an Ulster spacecraft.

Civil Wars

'We are here, in the providence of God, Protestants and Roman Catholics, side by side in a small country. It must be that we are here not to destroy one another, but, while we have opportunity, to help one another . . . '
— *John Frederick MacNeice, D.D.*
Bishop of Down

UNAPPROVED

After zigzagging for an hour,
exasperated, we spot an old farmer
who leans his head into the car.

'You could go down this way,
or you might chance the other,
divil the differ, providing that

you don't meet up with the boys
in black, or the British Army,
there'll be damn all bother.

I always take the Unapproved;
the cows prefer it: there's a power
of thick grass on *that* Long Acre.

Besides, it's only a dander.
With luck, you'll meet nothing worse
nor Sara Clarke's old gander.'

INTERNMENT

A dawn sweep through Altamuskin.
A survivor of the '50s campaign
('That renegade, that turncoat — MacLiam!')
Is first on the list, lifted again:

A Presbyterian, still hewing to that '98 dream,
That pale blue light on the hills of Antrim.

MacRory shakes his grey poll, rubs his chin:
'If this goes on, we'll have to go to the barn
To take down those rusty pikes again.'

SHADOW

Across these lands a shadow grows longer,
the mortuary visage of Margaret Thatcher,
flushed with righteous anger,
a games mistress, a grocer's daughter,
her thumb on the scales of justice

Satisfied that her name is linked forever
with lengthening dole queues, humiliated miners,
riot-rended football terraces, that absurd Armada,
and the dying hunger strikers
who wrought that Iron Lady

Into their chief recruiting officer.

SANDS

This is a song of silence.
This is the sound of the bone
breaking through the skin
of a slowly wasting man.
This is the sound of his death;
but, turn the hourglass,
also of his living on.

PLACE NAMES

The convoy lumbers towards
Fál Bán: the white hedge.
A trip wire is triggered:
Hawthorn splashed with scarlet!
Fál Dearg: the red hedge?

WEEDS

March and counter-march
as jagged orange of whin,
thick rushy green begin
again to overcome our fields.

Each year we try to scythe,
hack, or burn them down,
knowing full well that next Spring
the same dumb stubborn
roots will stir underground.

A RESPONSE TO OMAGH

All I can do is curse, complain.
Who can endorse such violent men?
As history creaks on its bloody hinge
and the unspeakable is done again.

With no peace after the deluge,
no ease after the storm;
we learn to live inside ruin
like a second home.

SUNNY JIM

Sweet drunken father,
abide with me now,
guide my pen finger;
forget your anger!
Once, side by side,
we rested, felled
by a double hangover:

And you solemnly
told me that when
Simon the Cyrene
lifted the wood from
the bruised, raw shoulders
of the stumbling Christ
'twas light as a feather.

As may your burden
now finally seem!
Laid out upon
your second last bed
in the long brown
robes of the Third
Order of St Francis,

All the ravages
of those Brooklyn years —
old nickel pusher,
rough bar haunter —
smoothed suddenly away
to Dante's bony visage.
Your faith I envy,

Your fierce politics I decry.
May we sing together
someday, Sunny Jim,
over what you might
still call the final shoot-out:
for me, saving your absence,
a healing agreement.

Magic Carpet

I have been up here for days.
No, let's be exact, I have been
up here for months, for half
a year nearly, dreaming time
had finally stopped, meanness
been put to rout, the world
become safe for lovers, poets

and all the rest of us, as well
as we had ever wanted. No need
to bus-taxi trudge to the airport,
just step on that magic carpet,
from Cork to upstate New York,
from Altcloghfin to Albany, dream-
ing a haven that is suddenly real.

No need even to uncork the bottle,
with this private source of ambrosia,
up so high, it feels like flying,
a lifting of the mind's wings
with you beside me, on course,
luxurious as the Lee's coupled swans,
those abrupt gleams of the marvellous.

Yes, so high up here, so restful,
that all that toil seems meaningful,
and grudgery, seen properly, a cheer
of appreciation gone a shade wrong,
a hiccup of homage to the glorious process.
But is this paradisal gleam, this Dantean
spaceship, yet another form of deception,

this autumnal glow, a dangerous elation?
I tell you straight off, I am in no hurry
to come hurtling, or sailing down
as my little personal plane beats on, all
around me, such a snowcloud of lightness,
like a drift of swan feathers in a bedroom
that, control panel flickering, I start to sing.

Lost Worlds

At last, the parcel I have been waiting for:
I spread the Funnies across the flagstone floor
and clutching Teddy, dream float myself back
across the Atlantic, into my American self.

Blunt-nosed Dick Tracy, master detective,
the Katzenjammer Kids, those German street urchins,
Terry and the Pirates, the Dragon Lady;
later, Superman streaming through the air.
I thought Little Orphan Annie was a bore,
but big Daddy Warbucks adopted her.

The cattle shift in the warm, stalled byre,
my aunts ferry in the fresh frothing milk
to splash into wide-brimmed pantry crocks;
a chicken pecks at the back door.

Banished from Brooklyn playgrounds, by chance
I had fallen into my fathers' lost inheritance;
a child's dream of Eden, animals galore:
Tim nuzzling for sugar at the stable door;
but I would have bartered the ark of the farmhouse
for one celluloid squeak from Minnie Mouse.

Landing

for Elizabeth

They sparkle beneath our wings;
spilt jewel caskets, lights strewn
in rich darkness, lampstrings of pearls.

And then the plane tilts, a warm
intimate thrumming, like travelling within
the ambergris-heavy belly of a whale.

The abstract beauty of our world;
gleams anvilled to a glowing grid,
how the floor of earth *is thick inlaid!*

Traffic borne, lotus on a stream,
planes lofting, hovering, descending,
kites without strings, as I race homewards

towards you, beside whom I now belong,
age iam, meorum finis amorum,
my late, but final anchoring.

Acknowledgements and Notes

Acknowledgements are due to the editors and publishers of *At the Year's Turning* (Dedalus), *Aquarius, Céide, The Cork Review, The Cúirt Journal, Exile, The Honest Ulsterman, InCognito, Ireland of the Welcomes, The Irish Times, Magill, Ontario Review, Podium III, Poetry* (Chicago), *Poetry Ireland Review, Princeton University Library Chronicle, The New Yorker, Shenandoah, The Shop, Temenos, The White Pine Press* (Buffalo), and *The Whoseday Book* who printed the first half of 'Paths'.

page 51   Kamaladevi was Ghandi's adviser on traditional arts, the epitome of a sage.

page 63   Balor of the Evil Eye was a champion of the Fomorian race of giants, an Irish Polyphemus, and opponent of Lugh, the God of Light.